A Natural Education

Compiled and illustrated by Stan Padilla

The Book Publishing Company
Summertown, Tennessee

Book Publishing Company
P.O. Box 99, Summertown, TN 38483 USA
Copyright © 1994 by Stan Padilla

Library of Congress Cataloging-in-Publication Data

A Natural education : Native American ideas and thoughts / compiled and
    illustrated by Stan Padilla. -- Rev. ed.
            p. cm.
    ISBN 0-913990-14-0
    1. Indian philosophy --North America. 2. Indians of North America-Education.
            I. Padilla, Stan, 1945-
    E98.P5N384 1994
    970.004'97--dc20
                                                    94-5479
                                                    CIP

ISBN 0-913990-14-0

Let us put our minds
together and see what life
we can make for
our children.

Sitting Bull
Tatanka Yotanka

This book is respectfully dedicated to the Spirit and memory of these men who left a great legacy for all of us to follow:

Sitting Bull ◆ Tatanka Yotanka ◆ Hunkpapa Sioux ◆ Spiritual man ◆ Visionary ◆ War chief ◆ Defender of tribal sovereignty

Charles Eastman ◆ Ohiyesa ◆ Santee Sioux 1858–1939 ◆ Native American physician, Dartmouth College/ Boston University Medical School ◆ Author ◆ Social activist ◆ Instrumental in founding the Boy Scouts of America and the Campfire Girls

Chief Joseph ◆ Hin-ma-too-yah-lat-kekht ◆ Thunder Traveling to Loftier Mountain Heights 1840–1904 ◆ Defender of tribal Sovereignty ◆ War chief ◆ Spokesman

Luther Standing Bear ◆ Oglala Sioux 1868–1939 ◆ Educator ◆ Spokesman/Interpreter ◆ Attended Carlisle Indian School ◆ Published the book "My Indian Boyhood"

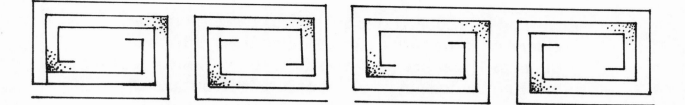

INTRODUCTION

Since earliest times there has been an aura of mystery surrounding Native American culture. Knowledge has been handed down from one generation to another through oral traditions: father to son, mother to daughter. While the ancient wisdom was encoded in legend, song, and symbols, the greatest body of Native history, philosophy, and life ways was preserved in the minds and hearts of the elders. Great care was taken by them to cultivate the memory of the past, to nurture and teach it in the present to prepare for the future generation.

With the coming of the Europeans to America, Native American life-ways were altered in a profound way. Education, as we know it today, was introduced, and the systematic destruction of the traditional methods for the transmission of knowledge was begun. Today these old ways continue to be woven with a small thread as compared to the past, but,...

they are still living!

For this book, I have gathered advice from the elders on "how to live a good life on this earth" and address the essence of a natural education: Education and Knowledge not born out of intellect, but out of heart, soul, and wisdom! Originally this book was prepared for Native American young people, but it became apparent that it could also be meaningful for many people, especially those who have become disconnected from their mother cultures. Please accept this book as a gift from the elders whose voices speak in the wind. Try as best as you can to carry these words in a sacred manner for that is their original intention.

Stan Padilla

All things are Wakan (sacred) and must be understood deeply if we really wish to purify ourselves, for the power of a thing or an act is in the meaning and the understanding.

Black Elk

Introduction to the Second Edition

We live in an astonishing world. Science and technology, in several generations, have catapulted us into instantaneous global communication. Computers record, draw, control other machines and even speak. And yet in the midst of all this twentieth century wizardry the time-honored tradition of the carefully spoken word as sacred continues. Stories, songs, chants, and prayers continue to help us to maintain a sacred way of life. The sacred word keeps us connected to our language, customs, and traditions. Understanding and meaning in these words give us purpose and direction in our lives.

This new edition of Natural Education has been expanded to again share with the world the wisdom of the elders. These words of wisdom were spoken at the end of the nineteenth century and can be helpful to us today as we begin our transition into the twenty-first century.

Let us continue to speak with love, respect, clarity, truth, and wisdom so that the whole world can be renewed in these ways.

Stan Padilla
1994

Before talking of holy things, we prepare ourselves by offerings ... one will fill his pipe and hand it to the other who will light it and offer it to the sky and earth ... they will smoke together ... then will they be ready to talk.

Mato Kuwapi (Chased by Bears)
Santee Sioux

What is life? It is the flash of a firefly in the night. It is the breath of a buffalo in the wintertime. It is the little shadow which runs across the grass and loses itself in the sunset.

Crowfoot-Blackfoot

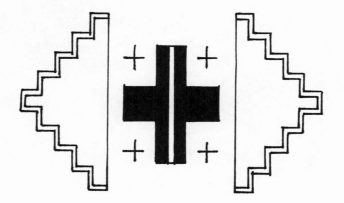

Knowledge
is like
the wind ...

once obtaining it,
you can go
anywhere.

Yellow Horse

Always do what you can, learn all that's in you, and bring it out for the people to see, especially the children so they won't give up along the way. When our heavenly Father created us, he gave us our minds too, not just our bodies. He gave us a great gift when He gave us our minds. Because our minds come from His, it's special; it's sacred. Our minds are sacred and we have a duty to it. Never forget this. Always do your best because we can. Our teacher is the first teacher and the leader of all teachers. So, don't say you can't. Don't hide your talents. Bring them out of your minds for everybody to see.

Essie Parrish
Pomo Spiritual Leader

From Wakan Tanka, Great Spirit, came a great unifying life force that flowed in and through all things—the flowers of the plains, blowing winds, rocks, trees, birds, animals—and was the same force that had been breathed into the first man. Thus all things were kindred and were brought together by the same mystery.

Luther Standing Bear
Lakota Sioux

All living creatures and all plants derive their life from the sun. If it were not for the sun, there would be darkness, and nothing could grow—the earth would be without life. Yet the sun must have the help of the earth. If the sun alone were to act upon animals and plants, the heat would be so great that they would die, but there are clouds that bring rain, and the action of the sun and earth together supply the moisture that is needed for life. This is according to the laws of nature and is one of the evidences of the wisdom of Wakan Tanka.

Okute
Teton Sioux

The Indian loved to worship ... There was nothing between him and the Big Holy. The contact was immediate and personal, and the blessings of Wakan Tanka flowed over the Indian like rain showered from the sky. Wakan Tanka was not aloof, apart, and ever seeking to quell evil forces. He did not punish the animals and birds, and likewise He did not punish man. He was not a punishing God. For there was never a question as to the Supremacy of an evil power over and above the power of good. There was but one ruling power, and that was Good.

Luther Standing Bear
Lakota Sioux

Everything is possessed of personality, only differing from us in form. Knowledge was inherent in all things. The world was a library, and its books were the stones, leaves, grass, brooks, and the birds and animals that shared, alike with us, the storms and blessings of earth. We learned to do what only the student of nature ever learns, and that was to feel beauty. So whatever came, we adjusted ourselves, by more effort and energy if necessary, but without complaint.

Luther Standing Bear
Lakota Sioux

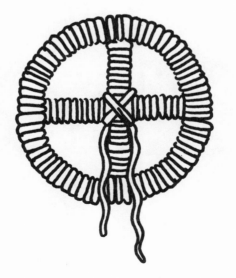

All living creatures and all plants are a benefit to something. Certain animals fulfill their purpose by definite acts. The crows, buzzards, and flies are somewhat similar in their use, and even the snakes have purpose in being. The animals roamed over the country until they found a proper place.

Okute
Teton Sioux

Animals and plants are taught by Wakan Tanka what they are to do. Wakan Tanka teaches the birds to make nests, yet the nests of all birds are not alike. Wakan Tanka gives them merely the outline ... All birds, even those of the same species, are not alike, and it is the same with animals and with human beings. The reason Wakan Tanka does not make two birds, or animals, or human beings exactly alike is because each is placed here by Wakan Tanka to be an independent being and to rely on itself.

Okute
Teton Sioux

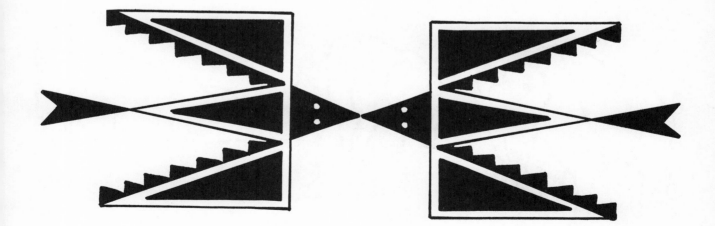

The Spring has come; the earth has received the embraces of the sun and shall soon see the results of that love! Every seed is awakened and so has all animal life. It is through this mysterious power that we too have our being, and we therefore yield to our neighbor, even our animal neighbors, the same rights as ourselves: to inhabit this land.

Sitting Bull
Hunkpapa Sioux

When we were created, we were given our ground to live on, and from this time these were our rights. This is all true ... We were put here by the Creator, and these were our rights as far as my memory to my grandfather ... These words are mine and they are true. My strength is from the fish; my blood is from the fish, from the roots and berries. The fish and game are the essence of my life. I was not brought from a foreign country. I was put here by the Creator.

Chief Weninock
Yakima

Remember ... the ones you are going to depend upon. Up in the heavens, the Mysterious One, that is your grandfather. In between the earth and the heavens, that is your father. This earth is your grandmother. Whatever grows in the earth is your mother.

Slow Buffalo
Blackfoot

The ground on which we stand
is sacred ground.
It is the dust and blood
of our ancestors.

Chief Plenty Coups
Crow Nation

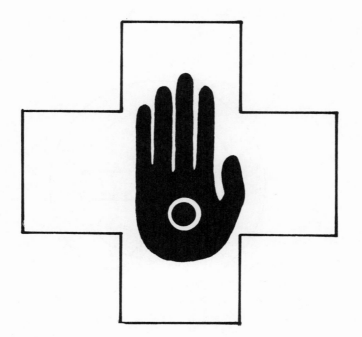

My son, never forget my dying words.
This country holds our father's body.
Never sell the bones of your father and mother.

Tu-eka-kas
Nez Perce

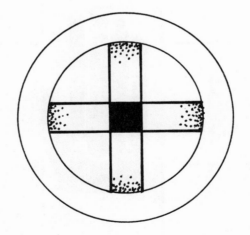

Mother Earth,

the trees and all nature

are witnesses

of your

thoughts and deeds.

Winnebago saying

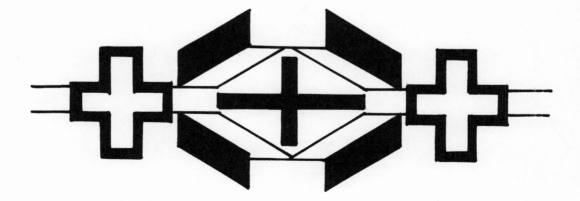

As long as the sun shines and the waters flow, this land will be here to give life to men and animals. We cannot sell the lives of men and animals; therefore we cannot sell this land. It was put here for us by the Great Spirit, and we cannot sell it because it does not belong to us.

Blackfoot Elder

If the Great Spirit wanted men to stay in one place, he would make the world stand still; but he made it to always change, so birds and animals can move and always have green grass and ripe berries, sunlight to work and play, and night to sleep; summer for flowers to bloom, and winter for them to sleep; always changing. Everything for good; nothing for nothing.

Chief Flying Hawk
Oglala Sioux

In the life of the Indian there was only one inevitable duty, the duty of prayer—the daily recognition of the Unseen and eternal. His daily devotions were more necessary to him than daily food.

Ohiyesa
Santee Sioux

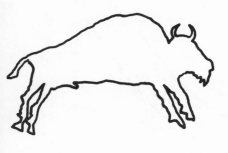

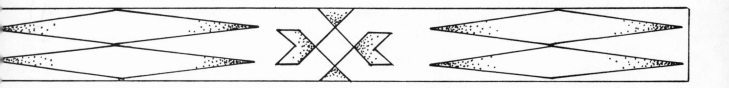

For the Indian kinship with all creatures of the earth, sky, and water was a real and active principle. For the animal and bird world there existed a brotherly feeling that kept the Lakota safe among them, and so close did some of the Lakotas come to their feathered and furred friends that in true brotherhood they spoke a common tongue.

Luther Standing Bear
Lakota Sioux

It is the power of the true Hopi People to unify the minds and spirits of all true peace-seeking peoples of the earth ...

The true Hopi People preserve the sacred knowledge about the way of the earth, because the true Hopi People know that the earth is a living ... growing person ... and all things on it are her children.

The Hopi Declaration of Peace

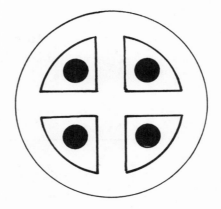

Look and listen for the welfare of the whole people, and I have always in view not only the present, but also the coming generations, even those whose faces are yet beneath the surface of the earth—the unborn of the future nation.

Constitution of the Six Nations

We were taught generosity to the poor and reverence for the Great Mystery. Religion was the basis of all Indian training.

Ohiyesa
Santee Sioux

The color of the skin makes no difference. What is good and just for one is good and just for the other, and the Great Spirit made all men brothers. I have red skin, but my grandfather was a white man. What does it matter? It is not the color of the skin that makes me good or bad.

White Shield

Each man
is good
in the sight
of the
Great Spirit.
Sitting Bull
Hunkpapa Sioux

We were told to treat all people as they treated us; that we should never be the first to break a bargain; that it was a disgrace to tell a lie; that we should speak only the truth; that it was a shame for one man to take from another without paying for it.

Chief Joseph
Nez Perce

Only the mind will make a person continue on. Only his will to follow those who are successful will bring him finally to his goal. Great wealth will not bring him all that way. Only his will to follow those who are successful. Whoever has very little must aspire to do as others around him who are more successful do. He must try to imitate, follow, and listen to those he wants to be like, and only in this way can he succeed in life.

Aleut Elder

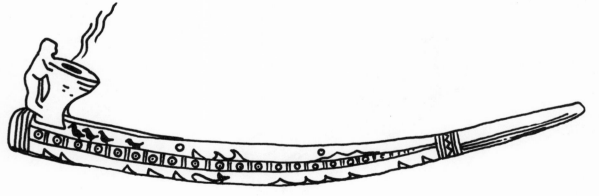

The Indian needs no writings;
words that are true
sink deep into his heart,
where they remain.
He never forgets them.

Four Guns
Lakota Elder

37

The man who sat on the ground in his tipi meditating on life and its meaning, accepting the kinship of all creatures and acknowledging unity with the universe of things was infusing into his being the true essence of civilization. And when man left off this form of development his humanization was retarded in growth.

Luther Standing Bear
Lakota Sioux

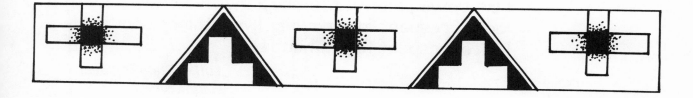

I know that our people possessed remarkable powers of concentration and abstraction, and I sometimes fancy that such nearness to nature as I have described, keeps the spirit sensitive to impressions not commonly felt and in touch with unseen powers.

Luther Standing Bear
Lakota Sioux

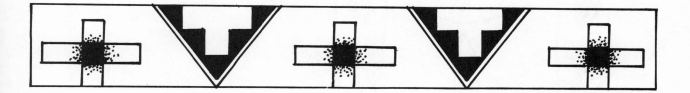

The old Lakota was wise. He knew that man's heart away from nature becomes hard; he knew that lack of respect for growing, living things soon led to lack of respect for humans too.

Luther Standing Bear
Lakota Sioux

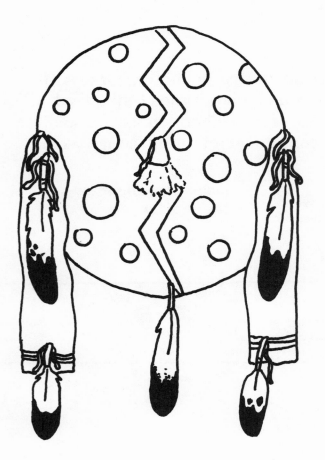

The man who preserves his selfhood is ever calm and unshaken by the storms of existence.

Ohiyesa
Santee Sioux

As a hunter and warrior, silence was considered necessary to him and was thought to lay the foundations of patience and self-control.

Ohiyesa
Santee Sioux

In the midst of sorrow, sickness, death,
or misfortune of any kind ...
silence was the mark of respect.
More powerful than words
was silence with the Lakota.

Luther Standing Bear
Lakota Sioux

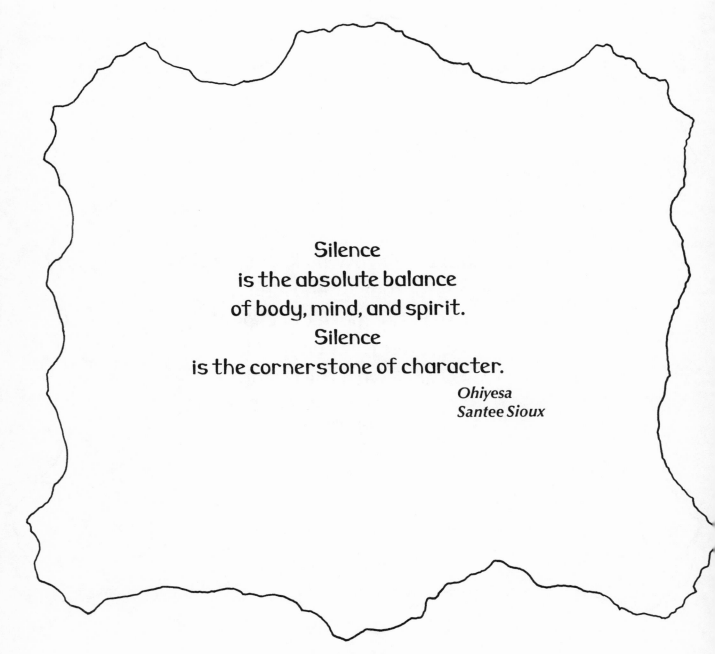

Silence
is the absolute balance
of body, mind, and spirit.
Silence
is the cornerstone of character.

Ohiyesa
Santee Sioux

It does not require many words to speak the truth.

Chief Joseph
Nez Perce

You must speak straight so that
your words may go as
sunlight into our hearts.

Cochise
Chiricahua Apache

My father went on talking to me in a low voice.
This is how our people always
talk to their children,
so low and quiet,
the child thinks
he is dreaming.
But he never forgets

Maria Chona
Papago

When I was ten years of age, I looked at the land and the rivers, the sky above, and the animals around me and could not fail to realize that they were made by some great power. I was so anxious to understand this power that I questioned the trees and the bushes. It seemed as though the flowers were staring at me, and I wanted to ask them. "Who made you?"

Lakota Elder

Sacred words spoken according to subject and purpose,
    and inside a house in the early morning
    before anyone has trodden the floor,
    or outside in the open air at a place
    far from the beaten track,
    where there are no footprints of man.
It is the usual thing
    that ordinary speech is not used,
    but the special language of the spirit ...
    magic words descend from father to son ...

Luther Standing Bear
Lakota Sioux

49

Conversation was never begun at once or in a hurried manner. No one was quick with a question, no matter how important, and no one was pressed for an answer. A pause for thought was the truly courteous way of beginning and conducting a conversation.

Luther Standing Bear
Lakota Sioux

Good words do not last long
unless they amount to something.

Chief Joseph
Nez Perce

Friendship is held to be the severest test of character. It is easy, we think, to be loyal to family and clan, whose blood is in our own veins. Love between man and woman is founded on the mating instinct and is not free from desire and self-seeking. But to have a friend and to be true under any and all trials, is the mark of a man!

Ohiyesa
Santee Sioux

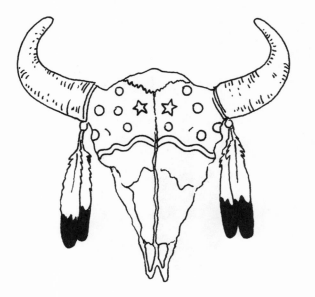

When you arise in the morning, give thanks to the morning light for your life and strength. Give thanks for your food and the joy of living. If you see no reason for giving thanks, the fault lies in yourself.

Tecumseh
Shawnee

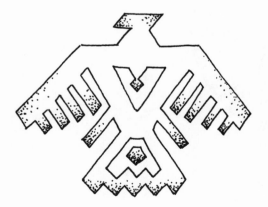

Training began with children who were taught to sit still and enjoy it. They were taught to use their organs of smell, to look when there was apparently nothing to see, and to listen internally when all seemingly was quiet. A child that cannot sit still is a half–developed child.

Luther Standing Bear
Lakota Sioux

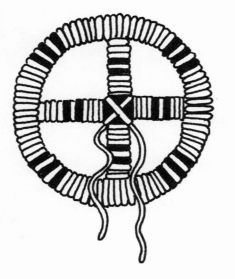

We thank the Great Spirit for all the benefits he has gifted us with. For myself, I never take a drink of water from a spring without being mindful of his goodness.

Sauk-Fox

Children were taught that true politeness was to be defined in actions rather than in words ... Young people, raised under the old rules of courtesy, never indulged in the present habit of talking incessantly and all at the same time. To do so would have been not only impolite, but foolish. For poise, so much admired as a social grace, could not be accompanied by restlessness.

Luther Standing Bear
Lakota Sioux

True wisdom is only to be found far away from people, out in the great solitude, and is not found in play but only through suffering. Solitude and suffering open the human mind, and therefore, an Eskimo must seek his wisdom there.

Igjugarjuk
Inuit (Eskimo)

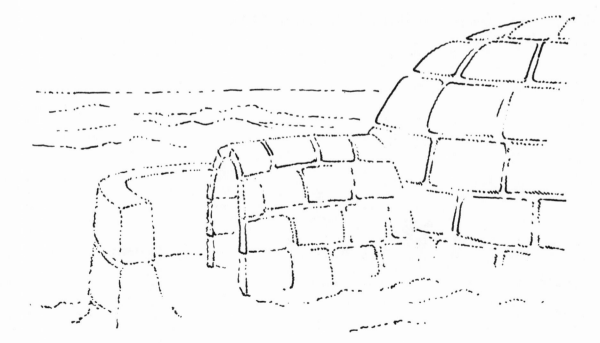

You don't ask questions when you are growing up.

You watch
and listen
and wait,
and the answer will come to you.

It's yours then, not like learning in school.

Larry Bird
Keres Tribe

Observation was certain to have its rewards. Interest, wonder, admiration grew, and the fact was appreciated that life was more than mere human manifestation; it was expressed in a multitude of forms.

Luther Standing Bear
Lakota Sioux

I have noticed in my life that all men have a liking for some special animal, tree, plant, or spot of earth. If men would pay more attention to these preferences and seek what is best to do in order to make themselves worthy of that toward which they are so attracted, they might have dreams which would purify their lives. Let a man decide upon his favorite animal and make a study of it, learning its innocent ways. Let him understand its sounds and motions. The animals want to communicate with man, but Wakan Tanka does not intend they shall do so directly—man must do the greater part in securing an understanding.

Brave Buffalo
Blackfoot

Too much thought only leads to trouble. We Eskimos do not concern ourselves with solving all riddles. We repeat the old stories in the way they were told to us, and with the words we ourselves remember.

Orulo
Igluik Eskimo

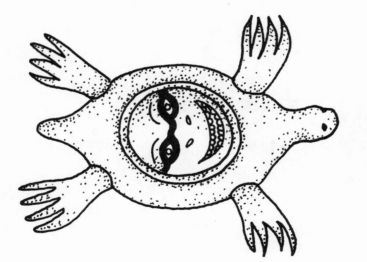

I still keep up the old system of teaching my children at the campfire. In the morning, I wake them up early and start to teach them as follows:

My children, as you travel along life's
road, never harm anyone nor cause anyone
to feel sad. On the Contrary, if at anytime
you can make a person happy, do so.

Winnebago Elder

Boys and girls began their education with their parents, and by the time they reached their teenage years, they had mastered the skills necessary to survive on the land here. From that time forward, the youth with his family and within his community devoted his attention to his intellectual and social growth.

Mayer Hobson
Inupiag Eskimo

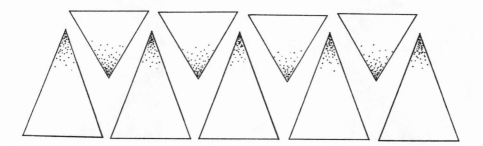

To the young the mother first teaches silence, love, reverence. This is the trinity of first lessons, and to these she later adds generosity, courage, and chastity.

Ohiyesa
Santee Sioux

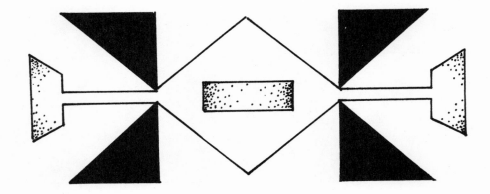

Lakota children, like all others, asked questions and were answered to the best ability of our elders. We wondered, as do all young, inquisitive minds, about the stars, moon, sky, rainbow, darkness, and all other phenomena of nature. I can recall lying on the earth and wondering what it was all about. The stars were a beautiful sight. Many of these questions were answered in story form by the older people.

Luther Standing Bear
Lakota Sioux

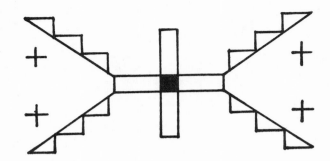

The old people came literally to love the soil, and they sat or reclined on the ground with a feeling of being close to a mothering power. It was good for the skin to touch the earth, and the old people like to remove their moccasins and walk with bare feet on the sacred earth ... The soil was soothing, strengthening, cleansing, and healing ...

Luther Standing Bear
Lakota Sioux

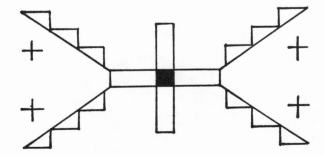

In our tribal custom, which was handed down to my grandfather ... each of his children were assigned to a tutor, like he had been by his grandparents, so that each child would be trained by an expert. It was not a parent that was undertaking the teaching of the young child. It was an elder. These experts were proficient in hunting and everything for survival, as well as teaching the blessing of the Great Creator.

Alex Saluskin
Yakima

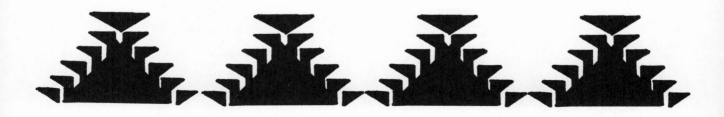

Try to do something for your people—something difficult.
Have pity on your people and love them. If a man is poor, help
him. Give him and his family food, give them whatever they ask
for. If there is discord among your people, intercede.

Winnebago Elder

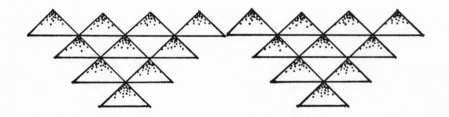

Regarding the "civilization" that has been thrust upon me since the days of the reservation, it has not added one whit to my sense of justice; to my reverence for the right of life; to my love for truth, honesty, and generosity, nor to my faith in Wakan Tanka—God of the Lakotas. For after all the great religions have been preached and expounded, or have been revealed by brilliant scholars, or have been written in books and embellished in fine language with fine covers, man—all man—is confronted with the Great Mystery.

So if today I had a young mind to direct, to start on the journey of life, and I was faced with the duty of choosing between the natural way of my fore-fathers and that of the present way of civilization, I would, for its welfare, unhesitatingly set that child's feet in the path of my forefathers.   I would raise him to be an Indian!

Luther Standing Bear
Lakota Sioux

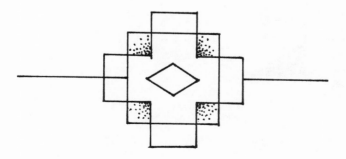

It is our belief that the love of possessions is a weakness to be overcome. Its appeal is to the material part, and if allowed its way, it will in time disturb one's spiritual balance. Children must learn early the beauty of generosity.

Ohiyesa
Santee Sioux

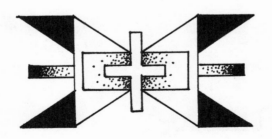

To clothe a man falsely is only to distress his spirit and to make him incongruous and ridiculous, and my advice to the American Indian is to retain his tribal dress.

Luther Standing Bear
Lakota Sioux

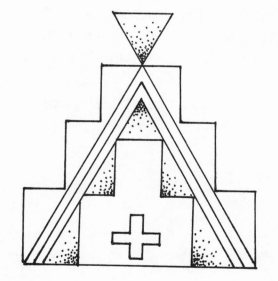

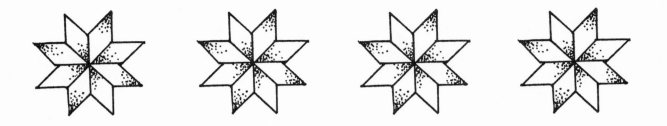

Hills are always more beautiful than stone buildings. Living in a city is an artificial existence. Lots of people hardly ever feel real soil under their feet, see plants grow except in flower pots, or get far enough beyond the street light to catch the enchantment of a night sky studded with stars. When people live far from scenes of the Great Spirit's making, it's easy for them to forget his laws.

Tatanga Mani (Walking Buffalo)
Stoney Indian

Grandfather, we know that in all creation only the human family has strayed from the sacred way. We know that we are the ones who are divided, and we are the ones who must come back together—to walk in the Sacred Way.

Ojibway prayer

Our forefathers struggled for survival so that we may enjoy what we have now. I should think the least we can do is to be grateful to them and remember what they stood for. We look back and see how they suffered, and here we are comfortable and have all the wonderful opportunities knocking on our doors. Be ready to accept these; your future is what you must think about.

Tom Ration
Navajo Medicine Man

See these elders, these are those who paid attention to this counsel, which is of the grown-up people. Do not forget this that I am telling you; pay heed to this speech, and when you are old like these old people, you will counsel your sons and daughters in like manner, and your spirit will rise northwards to the sky, like the stars.

Luiseño Elder

My words are tied in one with the great
mountains, with the great rocks, with the great
trees. In one with my body and my heart.

Yokuts prayer

It was the wind that gave them life. It is the wind that comes out of our mouths now that gives us life. When this ceases to blow, we die. In the skin at the tips of our fingers we see the trail of the wind; it shows us the wind blew when our ancestors were created.

Navajo chant

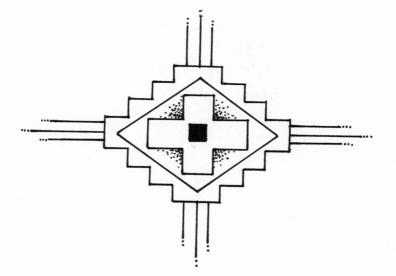

May there be happiness
May there be success
May there be good health
May there be well-being

In beauty happily I walk
With beauty before me I walk
With beauty behind me I walk
With beauty above me I walk
With beauty below me I walk
With beauty all around me I walk
It is finished in beauty.

Navajo blessing

Stan Padilla, Native American artist and educator, is author/illustrator of the book <u>Dream Feather</u> and illustrator of the book <u>Song of the Seven Herbs</u>.

He is very involved in the education of Native American young people. He is also active in the civil rights/human rights movement globally. He maintains an arts studio in the foothills of the Sierra Nevada Mountains in northeastern California.

These fine Native American books are available from:

The Book Publishing Company
P.O. Box 99
Summertown, TN 38483
            or
Call toll free: 1 (800) 695-2241
Please add $2.00 per book
    for shipping

Also available is a free catalog of Native American books, books on alternative health, ecology, gardening, children's books, and vegetarian and vegan cookbooks.

Basic Call To Consciousness	$7.95
•Blackfoot Craftworker's Book	$11.95
•Children Of The Circle	$9.95
Daughters Of Abya Yala	$8.95
••Dream Feather	$11.95
• Good Medicine Collection: Life in Harmony With Nature	$9.95
How Can One Sell The Air?	$6.95
• Indian Tribes Of The Northern Rockies	$9.95
• Legends Told By The Old People	$5.95
••A Natural Education	$8.95
The People: Native American Thoughts and Feelings	$5.95
Sacred Song Of The Hermit Thrush	$5.95
••Song Of The Seven Herbs	$10.95
Song Of The Wild Violets	$5.95
Spirit Of The White Bison	$5.95
• Teachings Of Nature	$8.95
• Traditional Dress	$5.95

• Good Medicine Books
•• by Stan Padilla